Chas Addams™

HALF-BAKED COOKBOOK

Simon & Schuster

New York   London   Toronto   Sydney

For
Tee

Merry Xmas
1973

Café Styx

One evening several years ago as I was dining on raw oysters, sea snails, and sea urchins at the Café de Turin in Nice, I found myself seated opposite an elderly and rather curious man—part Mediterranean, part bird, part satyr—who wasn't at all familiar with the many varieties of seafood that surrounded him. He would inquire as to whether a particular dish was good, and when his interlocutor endorsed it—which was always the case—he would order a generous portion. He had a terrific appetite and a wonderful manner of curving his thin body so that his beaked face would bow before his dish, as if to better relish the delicacies he was about to enjoy, or perhaps pay homage to them. He was still voraciously eating when I got up to leave, and as I reached the door, he turned to one of his neighbors and began a tale of which I was to hear only the first few words: "There was a man who ate everything on earth . . ."

Such ravenousness is not, however, always so joyful. Consider one of the most extreme, indeed apocalyptic, examples of incorporation, a case of paranoia recounted by the psychoanalyst Eugène Minkowski in 1923 of a patient, beset by delusions of ruin and guilt, who anticipates a terrible punishment that will come in culinary form. It consists of what he called the "refuse policy." This law, instituted especially for him, stipulates that all the waste matter of the world must be placed into his stomach: ashes, burnt matches, and cigarette stubs; crumbs, fruit pits, chicken bones, and the wine left at the bottom of the glass; needles and bits of thread, paper scraps, glass shards, nail parings, hair clippings, empty bottles, subway tickets, newspaper wrappings; dust on shoes, bathwater, kitchen garbage, cadavers of animals and people. The egg, he insists, is his worst enemy because of the shell. He finally realizes that a clock is nothing but key, case, hands, cogs, springs, weights, et cetera, all awaiting disassembly, all potential garbage. Everything, absolutely everything, is meant for his anguished consumption. His fate was to become a black hole that would devour the entire universe.

The culinary humor of Charles Addams vacillates between these two anecdotes: between joyful wisdom and anguished recognition, between an uncanny joie de vivre and an ineluctable morbidity.

For cuisine is a fundamentally eerie process, the artistic transformation of death into life. But Addams—with the circumvention of logical reasoning, the pleasure in lifting inhibitions, and the sudden revelation of things long repressed that Freud has shown to be at the core of wit—reveals that sometimes the tables are turned on us, and that it is we who might well constitute the next course. The profoundest recognition is that of the finality of human existence, when we in turn become food for worms. Yet to make light of death is perhaps the only way to beat the Devil, and Addams accomplishes this with astonishing brio and hilarity, all the while evincing a true passion for things gastronomic.

Consider one example: the recurrent theme of the blackbird. His drawing of a king at table being served a pie and exclaiming, "Hold on! Is this another one of those blackbird deals?" is a masterpiece of culinary humor. The mainspring of the joke is the immediately recognizable reference to the famous nursery rhyme:

> Sing a song of sixpence,
> A pocketful of rye,
> Four and twenty blackbirds,
> Baked in a pie;
> When the pie was opened,
> The birds began to sing;
> Now wasn't that a dainty dish
> To set before a king?

Though blackbird pies are highly uncommon, they do exist. *Mrs. Beeton's Dictionary of Everyday Cookery* (1865) offers a recipe, and *The Oxford Companion to Food* (1999) indicates that such pies are still made in certain regions of Europe. Most hunting cookbooks will confirm this, and Roger Vaultier, in his classic *Chasseurs et Gourmets* (1951), gives three blackbird recipes, citing the Marquis de Cambacérès, famed nineteenth-century gastronome, who claims that the Corsican blackbird is a great delicacy. However, it is not the reality of blackbird cuisine but its role in the culinary imagination that is of interest here. The deeper aesthetic allusions of the drawing are much more complex, and its analysis will lead us deep into the cultural history of food. It is as if each drawing in the *Chas Addams Half-Baked Cookbook* suggested a recipe, to be subsequently examined gastronomically. Let us therefore consider blackbird pies in the dual context of the nursery rhyme and the cartoon.

Astonishment. The fact that living, singing blackbirds emerge from the pie indicates that this dish is what is known as a subtlety, an ingenious culinary device characterized by its decorative prowess and its capacity to surprise—just like a drawing by Charles Addams. Such dishes, typical of Roman and medieval courtly banquets, received their most famous literary expression in Petronius's *Satyricon*, where at one moment during that summit of culinary ostentation, Trimalchio's great feast, a whole roast boar is brought to the table, and, as it is sliced open, live thrushes emerge to fly around the room; caught and cooked, one was offered to each guest. The comic absurdity of Charles Addams, most often based on the tiniest detail, can indeed be deemed a "subtlety," in all senses of the word.

Decadence. The morbidity of the blackbird, evoking sin and the Devil, is essential to understanding its symbolism. It would be difficult to write of gastronomy without mention of decadence, for excess and ostentation are of the essence of cuisine, and food has always been the most common form of conspicuous consumption. Famed among French meals is Grimod de la Reynière's "Funeral Supper" of 1783, when the young gastronome—who was later to invent culinary journalism in the early 1800s—staged his own funeral meal as a publicity stunt. Indeed, it was deemed so perverse that Joris-Karl Huysmans, in that bible of fin de siècle decadence, *Against the Grain* (1884), used it as the model for his protagonist's ultimate feast, an all-black meal that, though not including blackbird pie, consisted of tortoise soup, Russian rye bread, Turkish olives, caviar, pressed mullet roe, Frankfurt sausages, game in licorice-colored sauce, truffle coulis, ambered chocolate cream pudding, plums, grapes, blackberries, and cherries. In Huysmans and Grimod, culinary pleasure is subverted to reveal the rarely cited underside of gastronomy, that morbidity which is the key to all vanity. The disquieting realism of Addams's drawings brings this "black humor" sensibility to a new degree of wit and eloquence.

Inventiveness. Cuisine, like art and humor, is a great field of innovation. The fact that certain of Addams's culinary drawings refer to undesirable dishes, such as blackbird pie, or to things frankly inedible or even poisonous, is hardly an argument to the contrary. For culinary taste is extremely relative, and in any case, art is the domain of the impossible, or at least the improbable. Compare, for example, the recipe from Marinetti and Fillìa's *Futurist Cuisine* (1931) for a dish entitled "Words in Freedom," consisting of mussels, watermelon, chicory, Parmesan, Gorgonzola, caviar, figs, and macaroons, all arranged on a large bed of mozzarella—to be eaten by hand with closed eyes while listening to a Futuristic song by Fortunato Depero. This dish appears more phantasmagoric and provocative than gastronomic, and seems to bear a closer relation to the Futuristic plastic arts than to the history of cuisine. It is culinary invention pushed to the absurd. But sometimes the absurd is the source of the new, whence the bizarre modernism of Charles Addams.

Terror. Except in times of famine or penury, or in certain pathological conditions, food is usually associated with comfort and pleasure. But when the specter of the eater being eaten arises, cuisine touches upon the monstrous and the grotesque, the terror and the sublime. The second stanza of our nursery rhyme ends on a darker note:

> The maid was in the garden
> Hanging out the clothes.
> Along came a blackbird,
> And snipped off her nose.

Though this image is truly "addamsesque," to my knowledge it never served as the basis for one of his cartoons, most probably because this stanza, much less well known than the previous one, would offer too obscure an allusion. It also makes us realize that birds are not the best agents of cosmic vengeance, Prometheus's eagle and Hitchcock's *The Birds* notwithstanding. Considerably more horrific is the scene in Victor Hugo's novel *The Toilers of the Sea* (1866), where a giant octopus threatens to devour the protagonist:

> It is a pneumatic machine that attacks you. You are dealing with a footed void. The beast is superimposed upon you by its thousand vile mouths; the hydra is incorporated in the man, the man is amalgamated with the hydra. The two make one. This dream is upon you. The tiger can only devour you; the octopus, what horror, breathes you in! It draws you toward itself and into itself, and, bound, stuck, powerless, you slowly feel yourself emptied out within that horrendous sack, that monster.

Beyond the terror of being eaten alive is the ineffability
of being drunk alive.

Enough said—though you might well remember this scene
the next time you order a plate of octopus or squid. Hugo insists
that "at certain moments, one would be tempted to think that the
ineffable which floats in our dreams encounters, in the realm of
the possible, magnets that attract its lineaments, and that beings
emerge from these obscure fixations of the dream." Whence the
source of creativity in art, cuisine, and humor, all three of which
intersect in Charles Addams's aesthetic of the creepy.

Yes, all this in a blackbird pie! And the king, who has had more
than his fill, becomes, in Addams's adept hands, our jester. Today,
when books abound on cannibal and Paleolithic cuisines,
forbidden foods and roadkill recipes, edible architecture and
culinary theater, the drawings of Charles Addams hold a special
place. I would like to end emblematically, and reveal one of my
own culinary secrets: I always put a pinch of cayenne pepper in
my cream sauces, to complicate things by adding a hint of the
piquant to the richness of the dish. One might say that this is also
the secret of Charles Addams, who always adds a touch of the
macabre to his culinary drawings, so as to accentuate the spice of
life.

Allen S. Weiss
January 2005
Author of *Feast and Folly* and
How to Cook a Phoenix

"You telephone *Better Homes & Gardens.* I'll start making the hollandaise."

"This looks like a good spot."

Mushrooms Fester

SERVES 8

24 small mushrooms

Fresh lime juice

4 tablespoons butter

2 tablespoons fresh parsley

1/2 clove garlic

Grated onion, salt, pepper

2 tablespoons of the blood of a hare (or substitute sherry)

1/2 cup brown bread crumbs

Remove stems and sprinkle lime juice on each cap. Mince mushroom stems and sauté in butter until cooked. Mix all ingredients except hare's blood (or sherry). This to be added to moisten mixture. Put stuffing into mushroom caps and sprinkle with bread crumbs. Bake in 350° oven for 20 minutes.

"Hey, Lois, I think you better hold off on the mushrooms."

"You forgot the eye of newt."

"It stopped giving avocados."

"Fill it right to the top, children—company tonight."

Macaroni and Oysters

Put 2 cups macaroni in boiling water—boil for 20 minutes.

Drain and dry 25 oysters.

Put a layer of macaroni in bottom of baking dish, then a layer of oysters.

Sprinkle with salt and pepper.

Cover with bread crumbs, dabbing the top with bits of butter.

Brown in oven for 20 minutes.

Then add strained oyster liquor to moisten and a cup of milk.

"May I borrow a cup of cyanide?"

23

Second Platter

"Now, don't spoil your appetites, kiddies."

"A cask of Amontillado, please."

"And now, some monosodium glutamate to retard spoilage."

"The recipe calls for four and twenty."

Black Puddings

The blood must be stirred with salt till cold. Put a quart of it or rather more to a quart of old grits to soak one night and soak the crumbs of $1/4$ loaf in 2 quarts milk made hot. In the meantime, prepare the guts by washing and scraping with salt and water, changing the water several times. Chop fine a little winter savory and thyme, a great deal of pennyroyal, pepper, salt, a few cloves, allspice, ginger and nutmeg. Mix these with 3 pounds of beef suet, 6 eggs well beaten and strained and then beat the bread, grits, etc., all up with the seasoning.

When all mixed, have ready some hog fat cut in large bits and, as you fill the skins, put in at proper distance. Tie them in links, having only half filled them, and boil in a large kettle, pricking them as they swell, or they will burst.

When boiled, lay them in clean cloths till cold and hang them in the kitchen. When to be used, scald them a few minutes in water, wipe and put into Dutch oven. If there are not sufficient skins, put stuffing in basins and boil covered with floured cloths and slice and fry.

"So far, so good. You took the flour and milk, and added the sugar, the baking powder, and the vanilla. You folded in the egg whites. Then what did you do?"

"How do you know you don't like it if you won't even try any?"

"Hold on! Is this another one of those blackbird deals?"

Transparent Pie

Divide 1 cup sugar, beat half with 2/3 cup butter and other half with yolks of 5 eggs. Combine these—then add beaten whites, 3 tablespoons cream and 1/2 teaspoon vanilla extract. Prepare crust in 2 pie plates, pour mixture in and bake at 300° till brown.

Boiled Salad of Fiddleheads

NEWLY SPROUTED FERNS

Pick a mess of 20 fiddleheads and keep moist until 1/2 hour before dinner. Scrape off the hairs and scales with a dull knife. Unroll coils if you can without breaking, as they must be cleaned. Chop off the coarse bottoms. Boil them whole for 30 minutes in salted water. A pretty dish.

"Now don't bore everyone by talking about your new diet."

"Don't worry about Robert—he's on one of his health food kicks again."

"It's marvelous. All you do is add water."

"All right, all right. Now you can lick the spoon."

Intermezzo

Dandelion Beer

½ pound dandelion root to 1 gallon water—boil it well and when warm add 1 pound maple sugar, 1 ounce ginger, 1 teaspoon vinegar and a little yeast. Very good for the digestion.

Influenza Punch

FOR CHILDREN'S COLDS AND INFLUENZA

Thoroughly beat up an egg, add 1 tablespoon syrup of cloves, 1 tablespoon cinnamon, 1 teaspoon lemon syrup and 1 tablespoon rum. Pour over these 1 tumblerful of boiling water and add sugar to taste. Stir well. Put in tumbler. Best taken in bed.

"It's going to be great. All natural ingredients."

"We'd <u>love</u> you to stay, if you don't mind potluck."

Stewed Pigeons

Carefully pluck 1/2 dozen pigeons, rinse them, wipe with wet towel and cut off the heads and feet: in draining them, take care not to break the entrails; save the heart, liver, and gizzards. Put 2 tablespoons butter in saucepan, let it get smoking hot and then put in the pigeons and brown them: dust over them 1 tablespoon flour, then cover with boiling water. Season with salt and pepper and simmer gently till tender. Meantime, shell enough peas to fill a pint measure. When pigeons are tender, put peas with them and continue to cook until peas are tender. Serve in deep platter with bed of peas.

"For that special treat, do what I do. Buy Kotts Doggie Dinner."

"That was easy, wasn't it? Now it's time to add the powdered bat wing and eye of newt."

Potted Woodland Squirrel

4 large squirrels	2 small minced onions
Flour	3 sliced carrots
2 teaspoons fresh tarragon	3 chopped celery stalks
Salt and pepper	1 cup white wine
Butter	1 cup chicken stock
1 pound black mushrooms	2 pounds watercress

Skin squirrels, cut into quarters and dredge in seasoned flour. Sauté in skillet until browned in the butter. Place pieces in Dutch oven. Add vegetables to skillet and stir briefly. Pour wine and chicken stock over the squirrel and scatter vegetables over all. Roast at 350° for 50 minutes or until tender. Serve on a platter of watercress.

"The recipes never come out the way they look in pictures."

"It's usually busier than this at lunchtime."

Fried Locusts

A most notable viand brought in hot, in successive saucers. Not unlike fried shrimp. The inside is removed and the cavity stuffed with spiced meat.

Hints for the Ill

Care should be taken as to the position of candle or night-light in place—So that it should not produce shadows which might frighten the patient. (Also bad wallpaper—hallucination)

"It's been taken care of, Miss."

Third Platter

"Cheer up, son . . . what you need is some nice seagull soup."

"I've told you a hundred times. Don't feed Grandma at the table."

"I'll wash, sugar, and you wipe."

"Not sacrificial lamb again!"

"First the bad news. Henry Von Schlegel left his entire estate to charity. Now the good news. He arranged for coffee and doughnuts to be served at this hearing."

"I'm worried about Annette. She eats like a bird."

"Nobody else has complained about flies in the soup."

"I'm taking you off blackbird pie, Sire."

Digestifs

"Hilda, you've got to give me your recipe."

"Don't you have the chocolate bars with the bitter almonds?"

Hearts Stuffed

FOR VALENTINE'S DAY

Hearts are economical to buy and there is no waste from skin and bone. A bullock heart should be boiled or stewed first. After washing, cut the heart in the middle to make a cavity to take the stuffing. Tie a piece of greased paper over the top. Roast or bake in the oven. Small heart about 40 minutes. Large one 2 hours.

Stuffing for Hearts

1 slice or bits of dry bread soaked in cold water—when soft, squeeze dry. Beat with a fork. Add 1 tablespoon chopped suet, 1 teaspoon chopped parsley, 1/4 teaspoon thyme and a little lemon rind. Season with salt and pepper. Moisten if necessary with a little milk.

"Another vanilla, Benny."

Ostrich Egg

An ostrich egg is considered equal to 24 of the domestic hen. When taken fresh from the nest, are most palatable, tho somewhat heavy. Place one end of egg in hot ashes and, making a small orifice in the other, keep stirring the contents till sufficiently roasted. Season with salt and pepper and you have a nice omelette.

Reindeer Rice Curry

4 medium-size onions	4 stalks celery
1 tablespoon fat	1 cup peas
2 pounds reindeer meat	1 cup tomatoes
2 teaspoons curry powder	6 small potatoes
4 medium carrots	Salt and pepper

Mince onions fine and fry to light brown. Cut meat in 1-inch cubes—cook 10 minutes. Add curry, mix, add rest. Add 1 cup water and simmer. Add salt and pepper while cooking

"It's going to be tough to top that."

"How about one for the road?"

"To . . . hell . . . with . . . yogurt."

Charles Addams was the creator of the "Addams Family" cartoons, which first appeared in *The New Yorker* and were the inspiration for the popular *The Addams Family* television programs and movies. In 1954 he was honored with the Yale Humor Award and a Special Edgar Award for "Cartoonist of the Macabre" by the Mystery Writers of America. He died in 1988 in New York City.

In 1999 his late widow, Tee, founded the Tee and Charles Addams Foundation as a not-for-profit organization devoted to educating the public about the lifetime achievements in cartoon art that are the legacy of Charles Addams. In continuation of a tradition with Simon & Schuster started by Addams in 1950 that resulted in the publication of nine books of cartoons over thirty years, the Foundation issued a deluxe edition of *The Charles Addams Mother Goose* in 2002 with the Books for Young Readers division. The *Chas Addams Half-Baked Cookbook* marks the beginning of a new association with the Adult Publishing Group of Simon & Schuster, Inc.

Credits

MUSHROOMS FESTER
A combination of adaptations from *A World of Vegetable Cookery*, by Alex D. Hawkes, 1968, and *New Things to Eat*, by de Salis, 1844

MACARONI AND OYSTERS
Pennsylvania Dutch & Their Cookery, by J. G. Frederick, 1935.

BLACK PUDDINGS
The Southern Cookbook, by S. Thomas Bivins, 1912.

TRANSPARENT PIE, BOILED SALAD OF FIDDLEHEADS, DANDELION BEER
Grandmother in the Kitchen, by Helen Lyon Adamson, Crown, New York, 1965.

INFLUENZA PUNCH
Invalid Cookery, by Pearson & Byrde, Calcutta, 1909.

STEWED PIGEONS, POTTED WOODLAND SQUIRREL
How We Cook in Tennessee, compiled by the First Baptist Church, Jackson, Tennessee, 1906.

FRIED LOCUSTS, OSTRICH EGG
Breakfast, Dinner and Tea, by Julia Andrews, ca. 1859.

HINTS FOR THE ILL
Our Grandmother's Recipes, compiled by Lady Algernon Percy, 1916.

HEARTS STUFFED
Tried and Tested Recipes, by Anne Booth, Gloucester, England, 1900.

REINDEER RICE CURRY
Frontier Formulas, by Bess A. Cleveland, Totem Press, Juneau, Alaska, 1952.

Simon & Schuster
Rockefeller Center
1230 Avenue of the Americas
New York, NY 10020

For information about special discounts for bulk purchases,
please contact Simon & Schuster Special Sales:
1-800-456-6798 or business@simonandschuster.com.

Designed by Sam Potts Inc.

Manufactured in the United States of America

1   3   5   7   9   10   8   6   4   2

Library of Congress Cataloging-in-Publication Data

Addams, Charles, 1912-
Chas Addams half-baked cookbook / Chas Addams.
p. cm.
1. Cookery. I. Title: Half-baked cookbook. II. Title.

TX652.A343 2005
641.5—dc22
2005051022
ISBN-13: 978-1-4516-9749-0

Printed in the United States
By Bookmasters